SHOCKWAVE
SOCIAL STUDIES

# Earth
# Matters

Library of Congress Cataloging-in-Publication Data

Morrison, Yvonne.
  Earth matters / by Yvonne Morrison.
      p. cm. -- (Shockwave)
  Includes index.
  ISBN-10: 0-531-17747-5 (lib. bdg.)
  ISBN-13: 978-0-531-17747-1 (lib. bdg.)
  ISBN-10: 0-531-15546-3 (pbk.)
  ISBN-13: 978-0-531-15546-2 (pbk.)
  1.  Ecology--Juvenile literature. 2.  Conservation of natural
resources--Juvenile literature.  I. Title. II. Series.

    QH541.14.M67 2007
    333.72--dc22

2007012405

Published in 2008 by Children's Press, an imprint of Scholastic Inc.,
557 Broadway, New York, New York 10012
www.scholastic.com

08  09  10  11  12  13  14  15  16  17
10  9  8  7  6  5  4  3  2  1

Printed in China through Colorcraft Ltd., Hong Kong

**Author:** Yvonne Morrison
**Educational Consultant:** Ian Morrison
**Editors:** Nadja Embacher and Mary Atkinson
**Designer:** Carol Hsu
**Photo Researcher:** Jamshed Mistry

**Photographs by: Alamy:** © LHB Photo (fenced cattle, p. 29); © Vario Images GmbH & Co.KG
(battery hens, p. 29); **Big Stock Photo** (light switch, p. 12; recycle bins, p. 18); **Courtesy of
Action for Nature/www.actionfornature.org** (p. 31); **Courtesy of www.devonshealtheworld.
com** (Devon and Jessica Green, p. 30); **Courtesy of www.freeplayenergy.com** (wind-powered
radio, p. 26); **Courtesy of www.freeplayfoundation.org** (Africans with wind-up radios,
pp. 26–27); **Courtesy of www.sollight.com** (woman drinking, woman reading, p. 27); **Courtesy
of www.usbcell.com** (rechargeable batteries, p. 27); **Digital Vision** (swamp cleanup, p. 21);
© **Duncan Walker/www.istockphoto.com/duncan1890** (cover); **Getty Images** (p. 3; pp. 8–11;
Los Angeles smog, pp. 14–15; pp. 16–17; p. 20; pp. 24–25); **Jennifer and Brian Lupton**
(teenagers, pp. 32–33); **Photolibrary** (smoke stacks, pp. 12–13; acid-rain damage, p. 15; landfill,
pp. 18–19; Earth Day, p. 21; p. 28; free-range hens, p. 29); Stock.Xchng (cattle in pasture,
p. 29); **Stockbyte** (p. 7); **Tranz/Corbis** (car exhaust, p. 14; hybrid car, p. 15; pp. 22–23; house,
pp. 32–33)

The publisher would like to thank ecohero award winners Chanelle Adams and Gabriela
McCall Delgado, and Beryl Kay of Action for Nature, for the photos on page 31, and Devon,
Jessie, Arlene and Michael Green of Devon's Heal the World for their photo on page 30.

SHOCKWAVE
SOCIAL STUDIES

# Earth Matters

Yvonne Morrison

children's press®
An imprint of Scholastic Inc.
NEW YORK • TORONTO • LONDON • AUCKLAND • SYDNEY
MEXICO CITY • NEW DELHI • HONG KONG
DANBURY, CONNECTICUT

# CHECK THESE OUT!

SHOCKER

Stuff to Shock,
Surprise, and
Amaze You

Quick Recaps
and Notable
Notes

Word Stunners
and Other Oddities

The Heads-Up
on Expert Reading

Links to More
Information

# CONTENTS

**global warming** a gradual rise in the temperature of the earth's atmosphere

**greenhouse gas** any gas in the atmosphere that absorbs heat and warms up the earth. Greenhouse gases occur both naturally and as a result of human activity.

**organic** (*or GAN ik*) using only natural products rather than chemically formulated products, such as pesticides

**recycle** (*ree SYE kuhl*) to collect and process used items, such as cans and bottles, so that the materials can be reused

**renewable** (*ri NOO uh buhl*) from a source that can never be used up, or that can be replaced

**sustainable** (*suh STAYN uh buhl*) able to be continued without long-term negative effect on the environment

For additional vocabulary, see Glossary on page 34.

Some words change their meaning over time. It was not until the middle of the twentieth century that *organic* meant "free from chemicals such as pesticides." Before that, its main meaning was "to do with living things."

Humans have always changed their environment to suit their needs. They have hunted, planted crops, and cut down forests in order to survive. As technology has advanced, people have looked for ways to live more comfortably. Many people now rely on products such as cars, refrigerators, and lightbulbs. These things often use a great deal of energy, or contain chemicals that harm the environment. People in many parts of the world buy – and throw away – more products than ever before. The things that we buy, use, and throw away shape our world, and may also affect the world of tomorrow. However, people are now becoming more aware of the environment and the **impact** of human activity.

Environmental problems are on the minds of many of us. We wonder what we could do to make a difference.

Are we causing **global warming**, or is it a natural occurrence?

Can we become less dependent on **fossil fuels**?

Meeting the demands of a growing population is difficult. There may be different ways to solve any given problem. This book explores some things we can all do to help protect the earth and its resources.

Polar bears are affected by global warming. Rising temperatures are melting their icy **habitat**.

## People Power

As people began to recognize the damage being done to the earth, they worked to protect the environment. Here are some of their accomplishments:

**1850s**
Areas in the United States are set aside for National Parks.

**1958**
The first national air pollution conference takes place.

**1966**
The building of a dam that would flood the Grand Canyon is prevented.

**1972**
The **pesticide** DDT, which kills many birds and harms other living things, is banned.

**1991**
**Ozone**-destroying chemicals begin to be replaced by safer chemicals.

**1991**
Federal agencies in the United States begin using **recycled** products.

**2000**
Europe bans the sale of gasoline that contains lead, which can cause health problems such as brain damage.

# Green Gardening

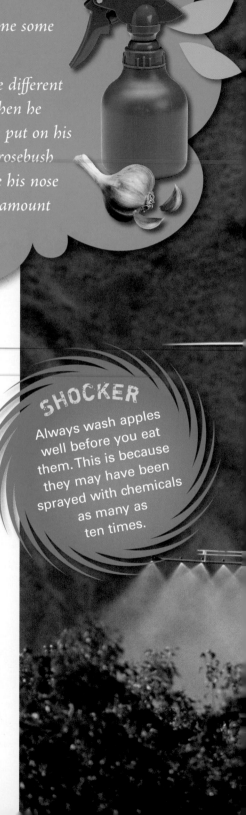

*Denzel's mother called out to him. "Can you grab me some vegetables from the garden, please?"*

*Denzel strolled out to the backyard. He checked the different rows to see what could be used in today's salad. When he noticed aphids chewing up his favorite rosebush, he put on his gardening gloves and face mask. Then he gave the rosebush a good squirt with the spray bottle. The smell made his nose wrinkle. He was still experimenting with the right amount of garlic to put in the spray to keep the bugs away.*

For years, farmers have used **synthetic** chemical pesticides. These chemicals kill the bugs that damage or destroy crops. However, they don't kill only harmful bugs; they also kill useful insects, such as ladybugs. These synthetic substances often stay on the food too.

**Organic** farmers use **botanical** pesticides. These contain naturally occurring chemicals. To fertilize, organic farmers use **compost** and animal manure. Organic fertilizer and pesticides are often better for soil quality and less harmful to the health of humans and animals.

Organically grown food is becoming very popular, although it can cost more. It takes more work to grow it, and the **yield** is often lower. Many people feel it's worth the extra money, because organic farming aims to have as little impact on the environment as possible.

SHOCKER

Always wash apples well before you eat them. This is because they may have been sprayed with chemicals as many as ten times.

Biological control is the use of animals, plants, and diseases to control other unwanted animals, plants, and diseases. This method avoids the use of synthetic products, but it can sometimes lead to other problems.

In 1935, cane toads were brought into Australia to eat the cane beetle, a pest of sugarcane. Unfortunately, the cane toads didn't completely get rid of the beetles. The toads bred rapidly in their new country, where they have few natural enemies. They are highly **toxic** and can kill animals that try to eat them.

## Green Fact

Botanical pesticides can also be toxic. Always read the label, and use protective gear if advised.

The overuse of pesticides and fertilizers can cause problems. For example, the runoff can pollute rivers and lakes, killing fish.

# Waste Not, Want Not

*Denzel returned to the kitchen and handed his mother the produce. She was chopping ingredients for a salad, which she was putting into a reusable plastic container. "Thanks, Denzel," she said. "It's time to get cleaned up if you want to come on the picnic."*

*Denzel and his little sister, Kaylene, went into the bathroom to brush their teeth. Denzel remembered to turn off the tap between rinses. He even turned off the light and the fan as they left the bathroom! It was easy to forget these things, but he was beginning to change his habits.*

Less than one percent of the earth's electricity production comes from **renewable** sources, such as water, sun, or wind energy. In most countries, the highest percentage of electricity is generated by burning coal or oil. Burning fossil fuels such as these releases **carbon dioxide**, a **greenhouse gas**, into the atmosphere.

Many other ways of generating power also harm the planet. Nuclear-power plants produce a lot of energy without polluting the air. However, the waste that nuclear-power plants produce is **radioactive**. This makes it dangerous to all life. Finding safe places to dispose of it can be difficult.

**Air pollution from a chemical factory**

**North America**

**Europe**

**Japan**

This map shows the world at night. North America, Europe, and Japan are lit up the most. The image is a composite of hundreds of pictures made by orbiting satellites.

## Green Fact

Energy-saving lightbulbs use 80 percent less energy than ordinary **incandescent** bulbs. They also last ten times longer.

## How to Save Power and Water

✓ Use energy-saving appliances. Switch off any appliances that you are not using. Don't leave them on standby.

✓ Put on more clothes when it gets cold, rather than turning up the heat.

✓ Dry laundry on a clothesline or drying rack, rather than in a dryer.

✓ Take short showers. Turn off the faucet while brushing your teeth.

Oh, now I get it. Part of this book is fictional, and tells a story involving conservation. The other part is nonfiction, and gives me the facts. This makes it both more interesting and easier to understand.

13

# Smog Alert!

*Soon the family was ready to go. For the short distance to the city, they would take their bikes. Denzel would have preferred to go by car. He liked SUVs. His mother loved driving big cars too. Unfortunately, they use too much gasoline. The family was waiting for an affordable SUV **hybrid** to come on the market.*

*Biking through their neighborhood was great. Downtown, however, they couldn't get away from the exhaust fumes. It was a relief when they reached the supermarket.*

Traffic is one of the world's major causes of air pollution. Vehicles produce carbon dioxide and toxic fumes. In some big cities around the world, the **smog** is so thick that people often wear masks while walking the city streets. Smog has been linked to asthma, bronchitis, and other respiratory problems.

Pollution is also dangerous for animals and plants. Chemicals in pollution, such as sulfur, can mix with rain to produce acid rain. In cities, acid rain can **corrode** metals and damage paint and stone. In nature, it can kill plants and pollute waterways, harming wildlife. Air pollution can drift around the world on wind currents. Acid rain often falls on countries that are not the source of the pollution.

## Denzel's Conservation Efforts

- spraying rosebush with garlic
- turning off water
- switching off light and fan
- riding bike instead of going by car

**Smog in downtown Los Angeles**

14

Sports cars and SUVs are notorious for being "gas guzzlers." They can, however, be made as hybrids, which run partly on electricity generated by the moving car. Other cars run on alternative fuels that come from animal or plant materials. These fuels are called biofuels. **Ethanol** is a biofuel often made from corn or sugarcane. Switching to biofuel is controversial. Some people are concerned that it could make food prices rise and lead to more forests being cut down.

This gasoline-electric hybrid car can travel 60 miles on just 0.4 gallons of gas.

Acid rain can badly damage or even kill trees, as seen here in North Carolina.

## Green Fact

Carpooling and using public transportation help reduce air pollution. Walking or biking not only produces no pollution, the exercise is good for you too!

15

# Shop Till You Drop

*In the supermarket, the family made its way to the fruit section. "How about oranges?" Mom suggested. Denzel examined a pack of six oranges on a tray wrapped in plastic. "These oranges have so much packaging," he exclaimed. "Let's buy loose ones instead."*

*As the family found the food they needed for the picnic, they avoided products with too much packaging. Finally, they made their way to the checkout. "No bags, thanks," they told the cashier. Their groceries fit easily into their backpacks.*

Many people are becoming educated consumers. This means that they think very carefully about the products that they buy. Every product in the supermarket takes resources and energy to produce. Even natural things, such as fruit, can take a lot of resources and energy to grow and transport. Most plastics used in packaging are made of petroleum, a fossil fuel. Manufacturing plastic products uses a good deal of energy. What's more, the trash that we throw out usually ends up in **landfills**. Over time, most trash begins to decay. However, some plastics, such as polystyrene, never break down.

**SHOCKER**
The energy used to produce a cornflakes box is greater than the amount of energy you get from eating the cornflakes inside it!

Waste that isn't recycled is either burned in incinerators or buried in landfills. Both methods produce harmful gases. Organic materials, such as garden and kitchen waste, make up more than two-thirds of our solid waste. If they are thrown into a landfill, they produce methane, a greenhouse gas. If they are composted, they break down to become nutrient-rich soil.

### Green Fact

Countries such as Uganda, Bangladesh, and South Africa have already banned the use of some or all plastic bags.

ORGANIC
GROWN IN MICHIGAN

Organic Braeburn Apples

$2.69

WHOLE FOODS   PLU 94103   PER POUND

Organic produce from the U.S. has a label from the United States Department of Agriculture (USDA).

USDA ORGANIC

### How to Be a Green Consumer

✓ Choose products that don't have much packaging.

✓ Bring your own bags from home.

✓ Choose locally made products when possible. This means that they haven't been flown or trucked a long distance.

✓ Buy fruit and vegetables that are in season. Some fruit and vegetables produced in winter are grown in greenhouses that use large amounts of energy.

✓ Buy food and drinks in recyclable containers.

✓ Buy **biodegradable** detergents for washing your dishes and clothes.

17

# The Four R's

*The family biked out to the park. A huge banner stretched between two trees. It read: Happy Earth Day! Lots of families were sitting around. Denzel and his family talked with neighbors and friends as they ate. There were three big recycling bins: one for plastic, one for cans, and one for paper. There was also a trash bin. Denzel's family had only an empty paper bag and orange peels to get rid of. They put the peels into a container to take home for the compost heap. Denzel lifted up Kaylene so that she could drop the paper bag into the paper-recycling bin.*

Denzel and his family are using three of the four R's of the environment: reduce, reuse, recycle, renew. Today, it is almost impossible to avoid packaging. That is why it is important to recycle as much as possible. Glass, cans, paper, cardboard, and some plastics are all recyclable. Renewing means replacing what you have used. You can't renew coal and oil, but you can renew wood and paper by planting new trees.

There is also a fifth R: repair. If something breaks, people often like to buy new products. But repairing broken things is less wasteful. It is also good to buy things that are durable. Unfortunately, many companies make products that are designed to wear out quickly. That way, the companies can keep selling new products.

**The Five R's**

- reduce – use less
- reuse – use materials more than once
- recycle – collect and process materials for reuse
- renew – replace what has been used
- repair – fix broken products

## Did You Know?

**Burn 14%**

**Landfill 55%**

**Recycle 31%**

The U.S. recycles 50 percent of its aluminum. If all the cans recycled in a year were stacked, they could reach the moon and back eight times!

In the U.S., only 20 percent of glass is recycled. Making recycled glass uses less energy than making new glass, because crushed glass melts at a lower temperature than the raw ingredients.

About 38 percent of paper trash is recycled. Making recycled paper uses 70 percent less energy and 60 percent less water than making paper from wood.

Only 5 percent of all plastic is recycled. Recycling one plastic bottle saves enough energy to power a TV for three hours.

Landfill sites, such as this, are often lined with plastic or thick clay to prevent toxins from leaking into the groundwater.

**SHOCKER**

On average, each person in the United States throws away 4.5 pounds of trash every day!

**How long does it take trash to break down in a landfill?**

Paper: 2–5 weeks

Leather: 40–50 years

Plastic bag: 50–1,000 years

Aluminum can: 200–500 years

Glass, polystyrene: 1 million years or more!

# Happy Earth Day!

*Soon lunch was over. It was time for the hard work to begin. The organizers began to hand out shovels to the* **volunteers**, *who spread out around the park and began to plant young trees. Denzel dug a deep hole. Kaylene ran over to him, carrying a seedling. She placed it carefully in the soil he had prepared. Together, they packed dirt around it. Denzel enjoyed having Kaylene along. Last year on Earth Day, they had cleaned up trash and planted grasses at a beach. Kaylene had had a great time squealing and chasing the little waves. He knew she would remember how much fun these outings could be.*

Earth Day is celebrated on April 22 each year. On Earth Day, people get together to plant trees and clean up wilderness areas, such as beaches and wetlands. Communities hold fairs and celebrations. They donate the money they raise to charities. Some people also hold protest marches to make others aware of environmental issues.

Trash on beaches and in the ocean is especially dangerous for marine life. Seals and dolphins can swallow plastic bags, or get tangled in them and suffocate. Seabirds can get them hooked around their feet. Fishing nets that are thrown away can kill marine life. Even fish can drown in them!

Kids in costumes made from recycled materials celebrating Earth Day

Great! I already know a bit about Earth Day. It's celebrated at my school. Reading is easier when you can connect it to something you already know about.

**SHOCKER**

Eighty percent of the world's resources are used by the richest 20 percent of countries – Australia and countries in North America and Europe. If every country used as many resources, we would need six planet Earths!

About half a billion people in 140 countries now observe Earth Day with volunteer activities, festivals, or protests.

# The Green Scene

The family had a couple of hours to relax at home before it was time to go out again. Denzel's grandmother always celebrated Earth Day with a big neighborhood party. She lived quite far away, so this time they had to take the car.

At his grandmother's house, the party was in full swing. She was involved in the very first Earth Day, back in 1970, when she was a student. Her friends from her college days still joined her in the celebrations every year. On that first Earth Day, they had all volunteered to clean up trash, plant trees, or help their communities in some way.

The very first Earth Day took place on April 22, 1970. Across the United States, 20 million people celebrated the occasion. Students from thousands of schools and colleges took part in nature walks, cleanups, and rallies. In the 1970s, more and more people became concerned about toxins polluting their air and water. Many people and organizations began to protest about companies that polluted the environment. They complained to the government. Sometimes the government listened. Many laws have since been passed to protect humans and the environment.

By 1990, Earth Day had become a global celebration. That year, about 200 million people took part.

In 1979, there was a serious accident at Three Mile Island nuclear-power plant in Pennsylvania. Many people became concerned about the safety of nuclear-power plants. One year after the accident, people protested near the power plant to demand its closure, but they were unsuccessful.

## SHOCKER

In 1972, only 36 percent of the nation's streams were safe to swim or fish in. Today, about 60 percent are safe for such uses.

People sometimes have difficulty understanding *percent*. It may be useful to remember that *cent* stands for "100," and *per-* means "by," or "parts of." So 60 percent simply means 60 parts of 100.

# Living the Good Life

*Denzel's grandparents had built their house together. All sorts of recycled materials were used to construct it. The rooms were designed to make the best use of natural light and breezes. His grandmother was proud of the house, especially because it produced almost all of its own power. The roof was covered with solar panels. There was also a rooftop wind turbine.*

recycled materials ——→ Denzel's Grandparents' House ←—— good use of natural light

Denzel's Grandparents' House

solar panels • insulation • wind turbine on roof

The sun has enough energy to power all of our needs for the rest of the earth's life. So why don't we use it more often? The problem is, solar energy has to be converted to a usable form of electricity. This is done using **solar cells**, which are housed in panels that are installed on the roof. At the moment, solar cells are quite expensive and bulky.

Wind energy is also all around us. The power of moving air can generate electricity. About 20 percent of Denmark's power is generated using wind energy.

In recent years, the demand for **sustainable** energy has increased. New technologies using wind and solar power are being developed and are becoming more affordable.

**Wind generators in the Netherlands**

## Green Fact

People have been burning manure for hundreds of years. Scientists agree it's a good idea. When cow manure breaks down slowly, it releases methane, a powerful greenhouse gas. Burning manure, like burning fossil fuels, releases the less-harmful greenhouse gas carbon dioxide. What's more, the world will never run out of manure!

**Solar-power plant in California**

## How to Build a Home That Saves Energy and Reduces Pollution

✓ Use **insulation** to keep in heat in winter, and to keep out heat in summer.

✓ Use energy-efficient construction that suits the climate. For example, to warm a house, install windows on the sunniest side. Build thick walls to keep in heat.

✓ Use energy-efficient appliances and lighting.

✓ Install solar panels for heating water.

✓ The temperature of the ground stays fairly constant. Use ground-source heat pumps, which pump water from the house into the ground and back again, to keep the house warm in winter and cool in summer.

Loft insulation

Solar panels

Efficient lightbulbs

Insulated windows

Wall insulation

Ground-source heat pump

25

# Green Gadgets

*Denzel's grandmother had made sure all her household appliances were energy-efficient. She loved gadgets, and all of hers were powered by solar, wind, or other forms of renewable energy.*

*"Look at what I've got, Denzel," his grandmother said, holding out her new radio. Denzel flicked the switch on, but nothing happened. His grandmother laughed. "You have to wind it up!" Denzel did, and was rewarded by a blast of music. "Hey, I heard about a laptop that can be wound up using a crank," Denzel said. "That sounds like a great idea too!"*

In the word *geothermal*, *geo-* means "earth," and *thermal* means "having to do with heat." Related words include: *thermometer*, *thermos*, *geometry*, and *geography*.

Power can be generated in many ways. We can use solar or wind power. We can use geothermal power, which is power generated using heat from under the ground. Or we can burn fuels. The problem is there are not as many ways to store energy. Batteries are the most common form of stored energy, but they are bad for the environment. They are packed with toxic chemicals that can leak into the soil when the batteries are thrown away. Rechargeable batteries last longer, so they are better. Some inventors are working on new technologies that could make batteries nontoxic or replace them altogether.

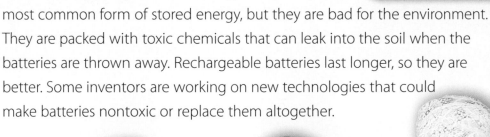

Some of the latest technologies are actually old. Windmills have been used by people since about 600 A.D. At that time, they were used by people in Persia (now Iran) to grind grain.

These rechargeable batteries don't need a special recharger. They can be recharged by being plugged into any USB port.

This bag is made from recycled sails. It houses a small solar panel that can charge up a cell phone, MP3 player, or GPS device.

This water bottle has a solar-powered light in the lid.

The Freeplay Foundation gives wind-up radios to people in developing countries who have no access to electricity or batteries. The radios help bring information and education to these people.

# Watch What You Eat

*Denzel took the radio outside to show the rest of the guests. The smell of fragrant basil plants filled the air. When Denzel smelled the herb, he remembered that his grandmother had planted it to keep the mosquitoes away. It worked! A friend of Denzel's grandmother offered Denzel a burger from the barbecue. The patty was made of ground chickpeas. He would have preferred beef, but it was still pretty tasty.*

Eating meat is a **controversial** issue. Many people rely on meat or fish to get enough protein in their diet. However, livestock need large amounts of feed. Sometimes they are fed crops that humans could eat. If humans ate the crops directly, instead of eating meat, more people could be fed. Waste from animal farms can pollute the groundwater people need to drink.

> I misread the word *rely*. I thought it said *really*. As soon as I read the next word, I knew that I had made a mistake. So I reread from the beginning of the sentence, just to make sure I maintained the meaning.

Eating wild fish is another concern. Many species of fish are now endangered because of overfishing. Fishing boats drag enormous nets that may be 80 miles long. These nets scoop up all the sealife in their path. Most of this catch is discarded, but does not survive.

Traditional fishing methods are often sustainable. These fishermen in Myanmar catch only what they will eat, so very little is wasted.

**SHOCKER**

About 40 percent of life in the sea has been destroyed in the last 25 years as a result of commercial fishing and pollution.

Cattle raised in large, spacious pastures can be expensive to farm, but they are often healthier than those raised in crowded conditions.

Cows, chickens, and other livestock are often raised in tight spaces in order to maximize profits. This increases the chances that they will catch diseases. To keep them healthy, they are fed **antibiotics**, which end up in the meat. **Bacteria**, such as salmonella, can become **resistant** to antibiotics because of their overuse in farming. Salmonella causes food poisoning, which is now more difficult to treat because some strains of bacteria cannot be killed with antibiotic medicines.

**Free-range hens**

Free-range hens have access to outdoor areas and a more natural lifestyle than caged hens. This makes them more expensive to farm, which is why free-range eggs often cost more than other eggs.

29

**Caged hens**

# Caring for the Planet

*Denzel had a great time at the Earth Day party. Discussion groups were set up to talk about various topics. Denzel's group had some younger kids as well as teenagers. They talked about whale hunting, rain-forest preservation, and solar power. Denzel enjoyed hearing what the other kids thought, even though he sometimes disagreed with them. The groups swapped ideas on projects they wanted to get started at their schools and in their communities. Denzel decided to help organize next year's Earth Day celebration. It was a great way to spend the day.*

Is it really possible to make a difference? Can one person help the environment? The answer is yes! All it takes is coming up with a good idea, then putting it into action.

Writing letters to politicians and companies can help them understand how you feel about an issue. When you write, be polite, and don't get angry. Clearly state the problem, why you care about it, and what you would like to see done.

Sometimes people won't listen. They are opposed to making changes. Some people think that changing takes too much work or costs too much money. The way to change their minds is to show them how they will benefit. For example, switching to energy-efficient appliances saves money as well as energy. Every day, many people make small choices that can make a big difference.

## Ecoheroes

Devon Green and her younger sister Jessica have their own business organizing recycling for more than 100 companies in Stuart, Florida. The girls have raised more than $250,000 for charities and nonprofit organizations. Devon says, "I love making a positive impact on people's lives." Jessica says, "Helping the environment is like helping everybody, because without our planet, none of us will have anywhere to live."

# Ecohero

Twelfth-grade student, Gabriela Delgado started a project to help protect birds and their habitats in Puerto Rico. When the birds in her neighborhood started disappearing, she became worried about the effects that big building projects in the area were having on the environment. Now Gabriela is teaching children and other members of her community about the importance of treating the environment with respect. She wants to help create a healthy environment for future generations.

Gabriela helps clear trash from Sonadora Forest in Puerto Rico.

Members of Hartford community help clean up.

Gabriela teaches third-grade and fourth-grade students about the birds of Puerto Rico.

# Ecohero

Chanelle Adams, fourteen, (far left) organized a major cleanup of her city of Hartford, Connecticut. She has helped teach others how to do the same in their communities. She has also attended youth environmental conferences in other countries, such as Japan and Germany.

31

Some environmentalists believe that all new home construction should be environmentally friendly. They think that the plans should be checked for energy-saving features, such as good insulation, solar cells, and ground-source heat pumps. They believe that we need to make such regulations. Otherwise most people will choose to take the cheaper option and build homes that continue to increase our environmental problems.

## WHAT DO YOU THINK?

Do you think that environmentally friendly building practices should be required by law?

## PRO

This is a great idea. Although the costs might be higher, people would save money in the long run, because their power and heating bills would be lower. Most important is that we have to put the environment and the planet first.

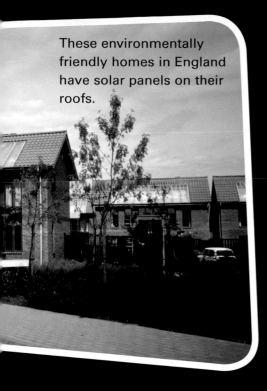
These environmentally friendly homes in England have solar panels on their roofs.

Other people feel that such rules would be unfair. They think that people should have the freedom to choose what sort of home they build. Building regulations might also make it unaffordable for some people to build a house at all. Some people think that governments should help reduce the cost of building environmentally friendly homes. That way, people would not be forced to take on the entire burden but would have the incentive to make the earth-friendly choice.

## CON

It wouldn't be fair if new homeowners had to install all these expensive devices in their houses, but people buying older houses didn't. People should have the choice. If governments really want people to make environmentally friendly choices, maybe they should offer them a discount on their taxes instead.

# GLOSSARY

**antibiotic**  (*an tih bye OT ik*) a drug, such as penicillin, that kills bacteria and is used to fight disease

**bacteria**  single-celled organisms that cannot be seen without a microscope

**biodegradable**  (*bye oh di GRAY duh buhl*) something that can be broken down naturally

**botanical**  relating to, or made from, plants

**carbon dioxide**  a gas that plants use to make food, and that plants and animals release into the air when respiring, or breathing

**compost**  a mixture of rotting plant material used to fertilize soil

**controversial**  (*kon truh VUR shul*) giving rise to disagreement

**corrode**  to destroy or eat something away little by little, especially by chemical reaction

**ethanol**  a type of alcohol that is used as a solvent and in fuel

**fossil fuel**  a fuel, such as coal, oil, or natural gas, that formed over a long time from the remains of plants and animals

**habitat**  the area where a plant or an animal lives naturally

**Compost**

**hybrid**  (*HYE brid*) having two different sources of power, such as gas and electricity

**impact**  the effect something has on a person or a thing

**incandescent**  (*in kan DESS uhnt*) glowing with intense light when hot

**insulation**  (*in suh LAY shun*) material that heat or electricity cannot pass through easily

**landfill**  an area where garbage is buried

**ozone**  a gas in the atmosphere that blocks harmful ultraviolet (UV) light from reaching the earth's surface

**pesticide**  a substance that kills pests

**radioactive**  material that gives off harmful radiation

**resistant**  able to survive the effects of a particular drug

**smog**  a mixture of smoke and fog that hangs in the air over large cities and industrial areas

**solar cell**  (*SOH lur CEL*) a device that converts sunlight into electrical energy

**synthetic**  manufactured or artificial; not found in nature

**toxic**  (*TOK sik*) poisonous

**volunteer**  a person who does a job without pay

**yield**  (*YEELD*) the amount of crops produced or harvested

# FIND OUT MORE

## BOOKS

Dubois, Philippe J. and Guidoux, Valérie. *The Future of the Earth: An Introduction to Sustainable Development for Young Readers.* Harry N. Abrams, 2004.

Inskipp, Carol. *Reducing and Recycling Waste.* Gareth Stevens Publishing, 2005.

Miller, Kimberly M. *What If We Run Out of Fossil Fuels?* Children's Press, 2002.

Morrison, Yvonne. *Take a Deep Breath: What Is $CO_2$?* Scholastic Inc., 2008.

Spilsbury, Louise. *Environment at Risk: The Effects of Pollution.* Raintree, 2006.

## WEB SITES

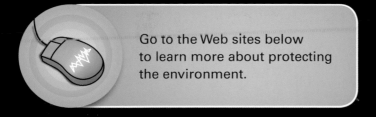

Go to the Web sites below to learn more about protecting the environment.

www.actionfornature.org

www.earthday.gov

www.kidsforfuture.net

www.niehs.nih.gov/kids/recycle.htm

www.organics.org/kids_club.php

www.nrdc.org/greensquad/intro/intro_1.asp

http://tiki.oneworld.net/sustain/home.html

# INDEX

# ABOUT THE AUTHOR

Yvonne Morrison has a huge garden and she's trying to grow her own vegetables without any chemicals. She says it's not easy, but it's worth the effort. The vegetables taste great! Yvonne lives with her husband in an old-fashioned cottage in a sunny seaside town in New Zealand. Her hobbies are dancing, listening to music, collecting antiques, and reading.